Let's Play Tag!

🔖 Read the Page

▶ Read the Story

🔄 Repeat

⏹ Stop

⭐ Game

😊 Yes

☹ No

💻

TO USE THIS BOOK WITH THE TAG™ READER you must download audio from the LeapFrog Connect application.
The LeapFrog Connect application can be installed from the CD provided with your Tag Reader or at leapfrog.com/tag.

For Susan Auerbach,
museum aficionada
—J.O'C.

For Sasha
—R.P.G.

Fancy NANCY at the Museum

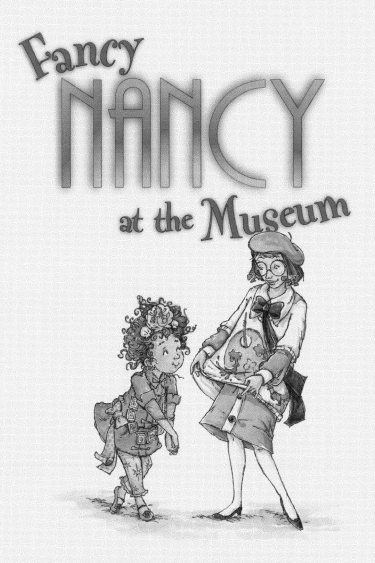

by Jane O'Connor

illustrations based on the art of

Robin Preiss Glasser

 Ooo-la-la!

I am overjoyed.

(That's a fancy word for very happy.)

Our class is going

to a museum.

I look extra fancy.

So does Ms. Glass.

"I love your shirt,"

I tell her.

Ms. Glass tells us,

"Today we will see masterpieces!

That's a fancy word

for great paintings."

The bus ride is very bumpy.

Bump! Bump! Bump!

Bree is my bus buddy.

"My tummy feels funny,"

she tells me.

Bump! Bump! Bump!

We stop for lunch.

Bree is not hungry.

But I am.

I eat my lunch.

I eat her lunch too.

I have two eggs,

 a juice box,

carrot sticks,

an apple,

 and a big cookie.

"*Merci,*" I say.

(That's French for thank you.)

Now we are back on the bus.

Bump! Bump! Bump!

"We will be there soon,"

says Ms. Glass.

I hope so.

My tummy feels funny now—
very funny.

Maybe two lunches was
one lunch too many.

"Ms. Glass! Ms. Glass!"

I cry.

"I am going to be sick."

"Stop the bus!"

Ms. Glass cries.

The bus stops.

Ms. Glass takes me

to the side of the road.

I get sick.

I drink some water.

I suck on a mint.

My tummy feels better.

But I am not overjoyed
anymore.

I am all dirty.

"I wanted to look extra fancy today,"
I say sadly.

"I understand," Ms. Glass says.

"And I have an idea."

We get to the museum.

"Come with me," says Ms. Glass.

I come out.

Ms. Glass's idea was spectacular.

(That's a fancy word for great.)

 "Lucky you," says Bree.

"I wish I got to wear her shirt and hat."

"It is a French hat," I tell her.

"It is a beret."

A man from the museum

takes us to a gallery.

(That's a fancy museum word for room.)

I love all the paintings—
the masterpieces most of all.
We see paintings of trees and lakes.
They are called landscapes.

We see paintings of flowers
and bowls of fruit.

They are called still lifes.

 The last painting is a picture of a lady.

"A painting of a person
is called a portrait,"
the man tells us.

"I like her hat and her fan and her beads,"

I tell the man.

"They are lavender.

Lavender is my favorite color."

(That's a fancy word for light purple.)

The man smiles.

"You are a very observant girl."

Then Ms. Glass tells us,

"Observant means noticing things.

Nancy is very observant, indeed."

On the bus trip back,

I do not feel sick.

I feel almost overjoyed.

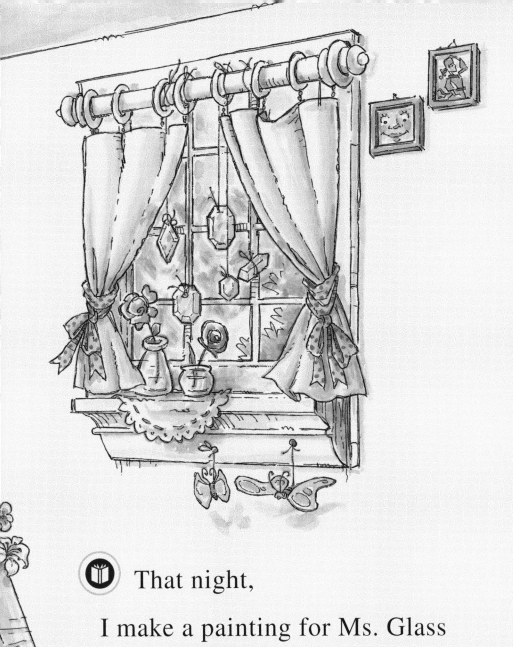

That night,

I make a painting for Ms. Glass

because she is so nice.

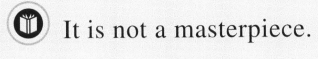 It is not a masterpiece.

But someday I will paint one.

Fancy Nancy's Fancy Words

These are the fancy words in this book:

Beret—a cap (you say it like this: buh-REY)

Gallery—a room in a museum

Landscape—a painting of nature

Lavender—light purple

Masterpiece—a great painting

Merci—"thank you" in French (you say it like this: mair-SEE)

Observant—noticing things

Overjoyed—very happy

Portrait—a painting of a person

Spectacular—great

Still life—a painting of things such as flowers or fruit